Library of Congress Cataloging-in-Publication Data

Poole, Scott, 1970-
  Hiding from salesmen : poems / by Scott Poole.
      p. cm.
  ISBN 0-9717265-2-3 (alk. paper)
  I. Title.
  PS3566.O6237 H53 2002
  811'.54--dc21
                                    2002151062

FOR LESLIE, RYAN AND KATHRYN

Also by Scott Poole

The Cheap Seats

LOST HORSE PRESS SANDPOINT · IDAHO

HIDING FROM SALESMEN

poems by
Scott Poole

pictures by
Robert Helm

CONTENTS

HIDING FROM SALESMEN

THE WAY WATER WEARS ON US

A man walks with a waterfall
cascading down his back. He wears
a plastic suit and a hat with a pump.
Moss has grown over his coat.
In the winter he freezes but keeps on
walking. If you ask him what he's doing,
he says every town should have a waterfall.
He got beat up the other day.
Punks smashed his pump and threw
his soft slicker in the river.
The people who watched
said his tears were quite beautiful,
astonishing
how they would not stop coming down.

WHY I LOVE MY GARAGE DOOR OPENER

I don't know if this a cure
for dumbness,
but I decided to grow corn

in my garage.
I dug up the floor, hung
special lights and slipped
in a tape of crickets singing at dusk.
I painted the ceiling black
and stuck it with fluorescent stars.

Then I felt smart, sleeping
in-between the rows, dreaming
of Kansas. But when the cricket tape turned
over to the whale side,

and I heard that sub-ocean groaning,
I felt dumb again under all that noisy grace.
But whales, I thought,
might dream of corn and that made me feel
smart and outrageously happy.

For hours I opened and closed
the garage door like the operator
behind the eye
of a great intelligent beast.

AFTER TAKING A PARTICULARLY GOOD NAP

Forgotten tulips on the bed.
An ant runs along the pillow.
You can hear the stream out back

where she bathes. The smell
of broken melon
rises up on the far side
by the window darkened with ivy.

Unseen, her satin dress
is in my hand, it's the fabric
within the fabric sliding complicated

between my fingers. Under the sheets,
my hand feels small
as though it could reach minute chambers,

places I'd put the word
"happiness" on thick paper,
frame it in a black frame:

the sky, the grass,
and her body's release
from the cold grip of the stream.

NO MOOD

I want to buy a Rodin—
one of those big bronze
man-with-hands-on-his-hips statues
which you know
everyone wants to put pants,
hats, ties on,
but I say no clothes, he's a statue you idiots,
and for a long time I just look
at ridges and bumps rippling there
but next to the TV in the trailer
is no good
so I put him outside
next to the abandoned dryer,
and that is a better aesthetic, I think.
Because I can still think sometimes
and so I bounce basketballs off him,
in the moonlight, remember . . .
and that is very nice
that sound, yes, very nice and . . .

                                        bong

it makes me feel like a shiny statue
and people try to put pants on him and me
and I say go away
we're in no mood for that now.

UNABOMBER, POET

I thought the man was a poet of sorts
when he tried to hang himself
with his underwear. Hell,
I'd never thought of that.

The fact that it didn't work
seemed even more poetic.
I'll never think of my underwear
in quite the same way.

He opened a new door
and looked out upon
reality's green backyard.
That's all I'm trying to do.

The next day
he told the tired people
in the courtroom, grizzled beard
flashing eyes and all, he wasn't
crazy, I can see

I'm going to have to work harder.
He's on television every night
and there's a website to find out
what his heart rate is. Meanwhile,

the families wriggle
and squirm in the courtroom,
and I can't even get my poems
into a magazine.

A WALK IN THE SPRING

Jumping around in happy May,
feeling the great stupid lust of Spring,
I accidentally stuck my leg in a coal mine
right up to the thigh.
Not a big coal mine,
but I thought it might be important to someone.
Miners made their escape
up my pant leg,
and I had to unzip my fly.
Several hundred happy men walked
out of my pants that day
and had an early lunch.
And you, who I was lusting after
asked "What the hell are you doing?"
It was hard to explain
the smile on my face,
considering my fly was open,
it was the middle of the day
and the bees were sucking
the rhododendrons dry.

A WOMAN CARRIES A GLASS HOUSE

A woman carries
a glass house.

She walks a little way
then drops it with a smash.

A few panes break—
glass sparkles down.

She spits on her hands
and this is great.

No one is watching.
A man tries to attack her,

and she drops
the house on him.

This is just fine.
More glass breaks.

The house is lighter.
She gains fans.

The woman climbs a mountain
into a hail storm.

Every window is breaking
to the dismay of the crowd.

Then, she sets the frame
on top of the mountain,

and it's beautiful and cold—
the view endless.

LOVE STORY AT MARVIN GARDENS

I love watching her gentle tresses hang
over the Monopoly squares.
She has just purchased a house at Marvin Gardens—
not the most exciting property, true,
but certainly a step up from my apartment on Baltic.

When I turn the block and tap at the window to say
I owe you rent, and I love what you've done with these flowers,
she says, "Save it.
Join me for this roast. I'm celebrating. I just won
second prize in a beauty contest."

Even though she's a beautiful second
and as we eat the roast no one is winning,
it seems that this moment is the elusive prize.
Some things don't need to be owned.

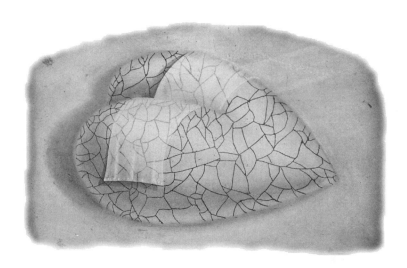

TURKEY IN PHOENIX

A man lures a turkey into his Subaru
and rolls up the windows.
It's Phoenix—the day before Thanksgiving.
Sweat is already forming on the windshield.
His family is coming. Maybe he could get away
in his little car of hope
if the turkey wasn't already in there.
Perhaps it'll be okay.
His sister's kids can sit in the backseat.
The adults can eat in the front and on the hood.
When the whole family is stuffed, they can go
for a drive, wear off the food and motor right
to the top of a red mesa and hug.
That might be nice.
The turkey looks nervously toward the horizon.

DUCKS AND DEATH

Walking to the river
with old popcorn for the ducks,
grass breaks
in the frozen brilliance.

They come out from under
iced branches of pines
like sleepy children
looking for mothers.

As they bend, breaking more grass
not apologizing at all,
I sense that death
can't completely inhabit the body,

that some part of us,
hand over its eyes,
must walk out still hungry
after it's over.

HOW TO HIDE FROM SALESMEN

You must keep your giraffe quiet.
Lie down, lie down
and curl up against that neck
on the cool rug of your August apartment.

Stick the legs out the window,
one set of hooves for each pane.
The tail will stir the leaden yellow air.
Try and convince the giraffe to be calm

though sirens rise
and small ears fold
though water boils over the stove,
and we try to forget

the savanna of trees and horizon.
Don't even think about the lions
or they'll never stop breathing
on the landing, knocking at the door.

AFTER THE VASECTOMY

Coming back, my bedroom seems changed
as if I have just turned the lights on
in the middle of a junior high dance.
The furniture stares back at me, caught.

The lamp I knocked over into the chair
earlier, foolishly excited, spilling coffee over the floor,
now looks like it's groping the overstuffed chair
and is desperately stuck in the minutiae
of an act it hasn't prepared for.

The wall which seemed so smooth this morning
with its white answer of "yes, you should,"
now has a startling acne of cracks and scuffs
blossoming fissures and weird bulges.

The clothes I threw on the floor so long ago,
as if the right shirt might make a difference,
now lie contorted on the floor
tangled with last week's pants. They dance,
frozen in grinding embarrassment
stiff armed and two dimensional.

In the middle of it all, the bed
with its sheets, books, glasses and toys—

the place where all hopeful things are planned
now seems like a poorly lit stage.

If I opened one closet I'm sure I'd find the pimply members
of a garage band; in the other, somebody's cousin
holding two fifths of gin.

All glare at me and ask,
"How in the hell, at age thirty-one
did you get in here
in that tight underwear
holding a bag of frozen peas in one hand
and a bottle of painkillers in the other?

GOING OUT

Maybe it's enough to be happy
like sunflowers in the snow.
Quiet walks up and touches them
with gray woolen light.

Maybe everyone has a little red head girl who
wears sunflower dresses in snow drifts,
blue boots skipping by brown barns.

We hear about people who die in the Rockies
on their way to Florida.
What the leaf stained highway said
went unrecorded.

Things still grow under funeral rain.
We can't stop
lifting heaviness among the flowers.

INSANE

Wouldn't it be nice
to be declared, finally, insane?
So you could get on with it—
throw the TV through the window,
drive the car
into an unpaved future
and walk around exclusively nude.
Imagine relegation to a warm bath in Ward Six
reciting the same Whitman line
a thousand times.
Oh to be unapolegetically fat
under a beautiful tree surrounded by guards.
If you love me
grab me here, by the chin,
in the dark,
put your tongue on my lips.
I don't care who
they say you are.
Swallow my breath.
Drool on me.
Tell me I'm insane.

OBSESSION

Next to the gas-powered chainsaw
and under a box of infant clothes,
swaddled in the bands
of an orange extension cord
I found a bottle of my old cologne.
The only cologne I ever owned.
The cologne from college.

It took a couple of pumps,
but I got the spray spraying again,
primed it really good
and leaned forward like a young mendicant
giving feeble thanks to my lord.

Then I tripped over my daughter's old high chair
and was sent stumbling again across rocks behind my dorm,
swinging on my leather jacket
over bony drunk shoulders,
sent flying out of my girlfriend's bed
into the dark leaves of some heavy potted plant,
sent laughing through that dorm room darkness

to finally reach this little bottle of Obsession.

Lying in the garage, my back releasing its full pain,
the engine of the lawnmower bending my spine,
I rose hoping she would appreciate this jerk,
now her husband, all his memories blazing,
walking back to the house.

A BAD DAY

I was at a bus stop
and suddenly wanted love.
But, there was only me
and the bus kiosk.

I looked for a love receptacle,
but there was only plexi-glass
and a wood bench.

Impossible!
All this waiting around
and no one considered our love needs?

A newspaper blew in.
I looked desperately,
but there was nothing in the news
I could manage love for.
So I waited
for love
to come to me.

I lay on that bench and waited
and even the bus never came.

TO THE YOUNG ROMANTIC

Your date is still kissing posters;
her perfumed coat a lamb staring into a fog
that has not yet inspired a landscape.
The car, still part of a mountain, has yet to be made.

This day is not a bottle of wine.
The night makes a poor corkscrew.
The trees may soon succumb to dinette status,
but relax. There is time.

The sauteéd garlic vegetables
are crashed out in their seeds.
The waitress hasn't quit her job
as an under appreciated movie extra.

The steak is scratching itself on a tree.
Your precious metals are still slumming
with the non-precious metals.
The pillows are busy swimming on a pond,

honking into empty air
like how you'll drive home some night, alone,
banging your head on the unmade steering wheel.
The pond itself is just tears still to be wept.

Don't check your watch. This will take awhile.
Love is still firmly attached to a dream
like an old tire floating down a river,
bumping its way through the rocks.

DOMESTIC SCENE DEPICTING A LOAF OF BREAD IN AN EMERGENCY

Sirens wail from a loaf of bread.
The brown cellophane is still.
The shiny gloss of the countertop is clean.
A butter knife reclines near
a butter dish, yet there is an emergency.

Sirens wail from a loaf of bread.
I did the dishes last night.
I even cleaned the oven, pulled the
racks out and scrubbed them down.
I made my lunch the night before. (I never
do that.) The coffee pot is clean.

Sirens wail from a loaf of bread.
I don't know, I replaced all the spices
in the spice rack with new bottles
imported from India. Each spice
bottle cost me a hundred dollars.
Look how orderly the spice rack is.

Sirens wail from a loaf of bread.
How could anything be wrong?
I ripped up all the linoleum this week
scrubbed, sanded, refinished

the underlying sub-floor then
laid down stone slabs from a Welsh Castle.

Sirens wail from a loaf of bread.
My kitchen was just featured
in *Better Homes and Gardens*,
Martha Stewart Living, *O*, and
Country Homes. Look at the red polished
granite counter tops, look at

(Sirens wail from a loaf of bread.)
the corner sink, note the original
woodcuts depicting important moments
in 18th century New England history.
The refrigerator was carved from
a Redwood for Christ Sake.

Sirens wail from a loaf of bread.
It took a team of Greek craftsman
eight weeks to lay the tile trim
around the mouth of the indoor
log fed adobe bread oven. Why the hell
is this store bought bread here?

Sirens wail from a loaf of bread.
I'll just light the cellophane on it
with this lighter. That's better.
Wow. Look at the flames jump.

Oh, crap the cupboards are on fire!
Where's the phone? 911. 911.

Sirens wail from a loaf of bread.
I can't even breathe through the smoke.
I think this is an emergency.
No, not the hand painted ceiling.
Escape. Outside. The sirens
are getting louder, the sirens!

FOR THE BROTHER I NEVER HAD

You would have had long hair
and liked to play chess.
You wouldn't have had freckles like me,
and I would have hated you at times
for that. You would mention to me
at a party when we were drunk adults
that you actually liked dressing as a nun
and prayed heavily
that no one in the family would find out
and after all that praying
figured you were a nun
so that's why you left the house
after your junior-year in college
to move to Taos to open a taco-ice cream stand.
(You know, ice-cream in the shape of tacos.)
Who would have thought
it would have attracted so many women
that would later nominate you Mr. Taos
and you would star in a charity calendar
with earthen wear and beads
strategically placed but not strategic enough
and that's why mother went into a rage
and threw the turkey out into the backyard
one thanksgiving when you couldn't make it home
and Dad and I sat there stunned

watching it steam in the pouring rain
and all we could wish,
now surrounded by our hunger,
was that you'd never been born.

MY NEW DOG

I love balloon animals, slick, transparent,
massive balloon animals. I want to live
in a cherry-red one, ninety-feet-tall.

I want to see the bees just try to destroy it.
I want the neighbors to leave beautiful
handwritten petitions on its gold collar.
I want to watch police lights bank off its curves
and crash back into the angled night.

If they come for me I'd like to be arrested
covered in small balloon dogs, to be dropped
so the dogs pop, to hear the neighbors ducking,
thinking it gunfire, substantial.

Later, I want to watch the whole thing on COPS
from jail, on a Tuesday night, on soft metal chairs,
on a TV hung from the ceiling in a plexi-glass bubble,
my life floating up there like a previous idea,
with prisoners who won't recognize me
or the fact I've already escaped.

A PERFECTION

There is no way to describe
the perfection of babies, I think
as I watch their almond eyes gather
and close, noiseless with love.
Then, I have to walk outside
and replace the starter in my truck.
I disconnect the battery, jack
it up, crawl under,
scoot into place on my back
with my tools.
Soon the various wires
hang from the engine like
frayed nerve endings. I reef
on the support bolts
then carefully remove the starter
heavy with broken parts.
Then checking the new starter, turning
its position, turning,
I try to remember it all in reverse,
lifting the careful weight of it,
turning the rusted bolts,
reattaching the unmarked wires.
I crawl out covered in machine oil
let down the jack, reconnect the battery
get in the cab, turn the key,

and
not a sound.
I listen for even a baby's cry from the house.
I walk back to their room, worried,
tiptoe, my hand festooned with cuts,
and they're so delicately asleep
I have to concentrate
to see their chests still moving perfectly
just the way they should be.

WHY I'M SUPPOSED TO LET IT RING

The way the woman on the phone
slowly says *Multiple Sclerosis Society*
with a gorgeous southern whiskey
drawl of long porches drenched
in bougainvillea and lemonade,
slow blues and torpid birds
lazy in long notes, I feel I must have
some sort of sclerosis myself.
I'd give anything
to help a society with a voice like hers.
Honey, take everything I've got.
Maybe it's the ninety degree heat,
maybe it's late and I'm long lost,
but you'll have to pardon me, this is love.

I EAT, SLEEP, AND DRINK THEM

—for Maggi Holbert

I wish my dinner table was a horse
but of course
tragic lovers would have romantic dinners
on it while I was in the saloon swallowing brass,
and no get away could suffice with a saucer for a saddle.
But Oh Nellie, what a beautiful blonde horse—my table.
If I could just head over the dessert, I mean desert
past the mountains, past the prairies, pass the potatoes!
Oh a horse of wood
could gallop me clear across the great ocean,
couldn't it?

CELLO

The fat man stretches till he's top heavy,
falls through an open window and lands in mud.
Getting up, his cigarette is covered in slop,
filter still clean. He tries to light the cigarette.
Nothing. He never expected reality at seven-thirty.

He reclines like a cello with strings of rain across his face.
A woman in a black velvet dress reaches across
his slumped shoulders and draws a bow over his chest.
Dirt crawls her hem. He plunks the cigarette
through the strings and fumbles to light it again.
Footprint pools shimmer with brown water
and shake as she zigzags to the top of a Bach suite.

How possibly important he feels!
Suddenly the hopeless mud is on fire,
and he is dancing the inhale, exhaling
a ballroom of pear shaped smoke.
Her breasts move like joy against his back
proving you can be happy anywhere.

WHY I WON'T BE BUYING ROGAINE

For the one day when my son
is about to run away steamed
in the fires of adolescence,
cracked with the fact that I'm his father
after he chucks a basketball at my head,

for that one moment
I want to leave the possibility
that a butterfly might land on my bald spot

unimpeded by a tangle of hair
so I might feel at the top of my thoughts
the soft strike
of a single small thing and all its fatigue,
falling from the angry air to rest.

For that second of forgiveness
from the grid of the driveway,
the lock and guidance of insults,
the terrible sun angling on forever
through the mist of insects
and the gravity of daily struggle,

yes, I will forgo all the hair in the world,
all the cool, combing, and loss of it,
to leave open this one clear spot
for us to smile and forget,
for even one wing flap,
how important we think we are.

BLAME THE LUNCH MEAT

The lunch meat's label reads "Smoked White Turkey"
and from where I'm standing this morning, hair on end,
it sounds to me like an insult from seventies cinema.

Sampling a slice, raising it from the unremarkable log
the turkey flavor says to me "Warhol":

Andy pausing over a silkscreen;
Andy happy in the moment of creation;
Andy leaving work to walk out on the fire escape;
Andy peering down a dirty Manhattan street in a striped shirt;
blonde hair, lazy eyes, deftly lighting up a joint
and blowing it into the steamed midtown air;
Andy observing a pedestrian, all maroon leather, bell bottoms and hair,
pause to look up at Andy;

Andy hearing "What are you looking at you smoked white turkey?"
Yes, this flavor definitely suggests

Warhol won't return to work today but instead will hit an early lunch
because of the pot, because of the inexplicable nature of insults,
forever linked to food—white bread, dark meat—
because this processed pulp is sometimes all we're offered to eat,
because this cargo of shit will not stop coming at us
the flavor clearly states we must protest and not work today.
And, I have to agree with the turkey. I'm staying home.
If someone calls, blame the lunch meat.

CAKE AT THE FUNERAL

It was a cemetery
in a box,
an old Halloween cake, fake grass,
headstones, and
because they were out of vultures,
a gnarled tree
with a pink flamingo
on a chocolate branch.

A man with one foot eaten
by an eager mourner
raked chocolate lines of corduroy Zen—
very peaceful.

And if you cut
the cake just right,
you might get part of a sugary corpse,
a jelly head,
some jigsaw of torso,
a gummy bone or bits
of toothpick coffin
ripping down your throat.

But with the red wine,
it went down fine
and when the stomach turned,
it turned to something better,
something like a celebration.

WHEN I WENT FOR MY MRI

First, I gave them flowers.
One of the nurses cried, the technician blushed,
nobody had ever thought of them before.
Then, I passed out chocolates.
The crew devoured them with giggles.
When the candles were lit,
they shut the door—willing
to break the fire code for this one.
After I popped the champagne, we passed
the bottle, chugging from
the long neck, letting bubbly drip
down our chins.
Then, I got naked. They protested,
but not for long.
Laid out on the table, I closed my eyes
and entered the throbbing circle
in blind and backward wonder.
All atingle, the circle began
searching for what was useful in me.
I let it register my love of baseball,
the friend I saved from drowning,
my way of driving through thunderstorms.
I let it register my bewilderment
in front of forests, and I hoped
something greater than me
might appear on the screen.

THE WAITING ROOM

For once, instead of plastic chairs,
a green park bench.
Delighted, he sat down with his unexplained condition.
One of the magazines featured a good piece
on the Impressionists. He felt so suddenly better
that he closed his eyes, one
then the other.

And when they called his name,
no one answered,
and no one cared.
So they called
the next unexplained illness
and the next . . .

When he woke
he was rested and could smell
pipe smoke drifting
from row boats
as women in straw hats laughed and sang
their way down the dim canal.

COLD ROOM

The moonlight is slick ice on my eyes,
and there must be penguins under the bed.

The light bulb is bare. This room is my own
frozen bowling alley in the world's attic.

Here, bowling pins pinch and squeeze the penguins
until they make bumbling love in the corner.

I can't help it. Now, I want to bowl and explore the Antarctic.
I rip the roof off the house. My bed seems enormous.

I want to die for birds that build upward into the black sky
so their shadows can strike across winter stars.

Beautiful awkwardness. I hear the planets rumble
as penguins pick up spares in the dark.

THANKSGIVING

A twenty-pound turkey on a paper plate
thaws in the kitchen.

The sheets fold across
the bed diagonally. The light
doesn't come, but broods—
a carpenter considering an edifice.

I lay my head sideways in thankfulness
and look at the crease where your leg
meets your body. Rolling my eyes
down your stomach, they catch

and pool in the center.
Bristles of the carpet scratch
the finger's edge.

Someone pulls a horse
alongside the world.

MY SUGGESTION

When the car broke down outside The Dalles, Oregon,
my suggestion was to get the spear from the anthropology conference
out of the trunk and stab the damn car several hundred times
in the tires, hood, lights, roof, trunk, windshields
and doors. I lamented that we didn't have a hundred spears
so we could leave them stuck in the car every time we stabbed it
thus giving it the look of a giant porcupine with wheels.
I thought we should get some hot oil from somewhere and pour it
over the top of the vehicle. Why not
beat on it with a shovel until it took the shape
of a giant metal head with wild spear hair?
Think of all the people that would pull over
imagining the giant melted head a "tourist event."
Consider the traffic, the police, the imitators
burning their cars in joy, the art critics, wine
& cheese events in the half-light of the canyon,
people in black milling about, talking about raw energy,
Renoir, Cézanne, Rodin, everyone French.
We could just hang out there
in the caves way up the canyon wall and watch,
eating popcorn and rabbits, making buffaloes our pets.
Oh would I love to ride a buffalo down the hill
with a six-pack hanging over its neck so I could huck
a can at a tourist and say "Gentle traveler. There's a special music

when you run your hand along the spine of a salmon."
Let's just attack every car that drives by with
spears, dynamite, and giant boulders like German deities,
and then run back to our ancient cave womb and
make love so beautiful it changes the shape of the planets.
She looked at me, then called a tow truck, thank God.

WINE AND CHEESE

I tried that already.
I took the bottle
and the cheese
down to the river
with her, and we
tripped over
the rocks and
branches
snagged her dress,
and we burst
out of the bushes
laughing . . . all that.

But, the river smelled of lost socks,
and the beach
was littered with empty wine bottles
hundreds of half eaten blocks of cheese,
dissolved crackers stinking up the scene,
broken row boats, torn lingerie
and picnic baskets full of mice.

Well—I sighed,
pulling a small cloth from a tree.

We stood geologically still.
A few gaunt birds circled above.
She was so beautiful.

MORNING SKETCH

got the jazz on
cooking sausage for breakfast
throw one out the window
see bird bounce to pick
it up
fly into the branches to eat
I'm flying too
you got my fingers up there
laying notes on the trees

COFFEE TABLE SLUMBER

I'm sleeping on the coffee table tonight.
I think someone stole my bed.
The modern coffee table consists of glass and wooden legs.

It's like living on a fortieth story window
glued by the night.
Dreams fall fast from my head
blossom on the pavement.
I feel like six gallons of milk
forgotten in the garage freezer.

I throw a white table cloth
into the elegant night.
The floor is beautifully covered with books
under which small passages run
for the work of spiders.

There's no where to put this drink.
The stars are too small for coasters.

CHECKING ACCOUNTS

I just finished running to the bank,
because my wife says the money
has got to be in, or we bounce big

when this man on the bus tells me
he won't keep his money in checking
because his old lady will get it

for child support—some lawyer will
find it and yank it on him.
He gets his check and cashes it

then and there. Don't use checking.
As he's saying this, we pass over
a hundred-year-old stone bridge,

and I fear
the bridge is going to fall chunk
by chunk into the sad Spokane River. I know

we all make it across though. Amazing.
He carries a big bag around with him.
He says it's his laundry, but who knows?

FLUORESCENT LIGHTS

I want to say lion.
I want to say mountain.
I want to say papyrus
left alone on white linen.

But, I am employed
at 7-11 and such vocabulary
does not lend itself to my occupation.

So, I say hot dog
or wrap my lips on coffee,
debit card, or what pulp
palpitates up from my heart.
So, if you, my secret friends,
walk into buy a soft pack of Camels
I will give you a great hug
with my small flickering eyes,
kiss you with a nod

and say silently
hot dog lion,
coffee mountain,
camel papyrus,
have a good day.

ED'S KNICK-KNACK CABINET

I was stacking mugs in the back of a truck
because that was what you were told to do.
They'd come off the line and you brought them over
one by one with gloved hands and set the glasses carefully down.
It might have been a decent job, but
we had to walk around with a cupboard on our chests,
a little wooden knick-knack cabinet, two wooden doors,
the kind they use for china cups. Yeah, I know. What the hell.
Frequently, the manager would walk up
and check to see if we had hid a mug in there.
If so, you were fired.
Some guys tried it.
Some guys put their cigarettes in there.
Some put in a little plan for the future or
some notes they had scribbled down.
Still, once every hour, they'd check your cupboard,
and if you were caught, you were fired. Strange as it sounds,
you got to keep the cupboard. I still have mine,
I keep my gun in it, over there, on the wall. Want a beer?

LOCATION

Driving home with one headlight,
eating free restaurant mints,
listening to my wife snore,
I wonder how many people
have been married at McDonald's.

People are always looking
for exciting and new
locations to host a wedding.

I remember this one
near a mountain.
I thought, who put this mountain
next to this McDonald's?

I imagine walking in, too tired to go
anywhere good and nourishing
and to my left are two gorgeous people
making the commitment of a life.

He has just cut his hair for the first time in two years.
She is tan and trim. They are both shaking.
The minister stands in front of the back windows
and looks happy at the people waiting to order
who have turned around to watch.

And behind him in the frosted etched glass
with the skier motif, you can see a thin cloud kissing
the peak of a snow crusted mountain
rising out of the centuries to join it.

I know I would suddenly want something different
than the convenience I walked in to order.
For the first time in my life, I'd walk out of a McDonald's
without eating,
the bright mountain rising above me.

And when you know exactly what you want
but you're not quite sure how to get there,
with one headlight, eating free restaurant mints
your wife sleeping on your shoulder,
that's the best.

THE SEXY SHAKERS

Shaker architecture is as simple as sex.
Two naked elms in a field wait to be
wooden bowls filled with light.
Each scratch visible.
Staircases. The sound of rising and descending steps
into clouds of bleached wood.
Rows upon rows of plain drawers without labels.
Skylit room.

All doors are open. The hinges greased.
Cold air dances without music.
A Shaker house is as sexual as a waiting skillet.

I don't care what you think.
The Shakers are the sexiest people.

All their chairs are empty.

NATURE PEOM XJ127H

A bear with a clipboard
counting salmon jumping through falls
leaden-white with the heavy noise of foam
reverberating into fir-lined cataracts,
turns toward me
and makes a mark.

That's the most frightening thing I could imagine
finding in the woods.

SIGNS OF CIVILIZATION

A group of eleven-year-old girls
in their soccer uniforms wait
for a table at Pizza Hut. They huddle
in a knot near the door wearing shin guards,
hair pulled back in pony tails, and it seems
they have been here since the dawn of time.

I have no problem imagining them equally at ease
near the entrance to a primordial cave,
apes shuffling in and out, bones dragging by,
an antelope struggling against jaws of a lion
not ten feet from an Adidas soccer cleat.

I have no problem at all
if they stand in front of me in line
at the Sistine Chapel with the hand of God
taking the pulse of their giggles echoing
against the weakening Italian plaster.

I'd find it very comforting
if I were to hike to the bottom of the Grand Canyon
and find them panning a gold stream,
discussing the goals they've scored
who's bringing the oranges next week
and what are best socks to wear during semifinals.

It wouldn't surprise me at all
if they were discovered, under
laboratory conditions, spinning
around an atom, kicking a ball between orbits
aloof, semi-giddy, distracted but cool.

In fact, it's just fine with me
if you invite them to my funeral. Let them
shuffle, talk, and pretend to act interested
at every entrance to the chapel. Let them run
around the casket practicing drills.

Please encourage them
to careen a ball off the minister.
Make sure they have plenty of Gatorade.
How bad could death be?
Go Tigers! Go Panthers! Lady Bugs?
Party of six? Right this way.

SINCERITY

—for the victims of 9/11

The first movement was walking, so people walked.
Then came the car, so the population drove.
Later, the jetliner arrived, and people filled airports and flew.

To walk costs almost nothing.
Driving is a higher commitment to a budget of gas,
insurance, cleaning, and repairs, yet, the common man
can manage it.
Flying is the most expensive of all, only a few
own a plane, and it's consider a luxury to just buy a ticket.

If you fall while walking, you can expect one person, if any,
usually someone who loves you, to help you
up off your bleeding knees.
If you crash your car you can expect a crowd,
bystanders, an ambulance, paramedics and police.
But, if you crash a plane,
thousands will rush in,
to help if they can, to know why
and soon the world knows and anyone
and everyone will wade through blood and jet fuel to help.

Workers, proud to be chosen, are assigned to pick each piece up,
then catalog it. No expense is spared, when cleaning
a plane crash, and the world gives freely to it. And if a single man
falls while searching the rubble for parts,
there is always more than one person there to pick him up.
It's the most sincere thing you've ever seen, the way
they brush him off, stand him up, and wait a second
to make sure he doesn't stumble again.

ACKNOWLEDGMENTS

Thanks to the many people who helped me with this book. Christine, who believes and perseveres against all odds and authors. Robert Helm for the great food, conversation, and his life's work. Joe Millar for making this a better book. Joelean Copeland for putting up with me. Chris for swapping poems on the plane. Ryan and Katie for giving me time when I needed it. Tod Marshall for suggestions and camaraderie. Tony Flinn and Dan W. for passing it along. Marty Demarest for giving me ears and an audience. Nance for her comments, even though they were stolen in Seattle. Jen Reid for reading the manuscript. And my most sincere love and thanks to Leslie. Nothing exists without you.

The author also wishes to thank the editors of the following magazines in which some of these poems originally appeared: *The Candle, Slow Trains, Smartish Pace, Gumball Poetry, Talking River Review, Redactions, Infinite Race,* M.A.G., *Blue Moon Review, Firebush, The Temple, Stringtown* and *Spillway.*

ABOUT THE AUTHOR

Scott Poole is the associate director of Eastern Washington University Press. His first book, *The Cheap Seats*, was a finalist for *Forward Magazine's* Book of the Year awards. He lives with his family in Spokane, Washington where his work can be heard every Monday morning on KPBX 91.1, Spokane Public Radio.

ABOUT THE ARTIST

Robert Helm is an award winning artist whose works have appeared in galleries as far flung as Seattle, Los Angeles, New York, Paris, and Berlin.